T0045028

WORLD WINDOWS

Things Made of Wood

HEINLE CENGAGE Learning

Y|S|G A YBM COMPANY Young & Son Global, Inc.

What is made of wood in your home?

Contents

Vocabulary	4
Wood from Trees	6
Uses for Wood	7
Pencil	8
Book	9
Chair	10
House	11
Paper Towels	12
Violin	13
Summary	14
Song	15
Index	16

Vocabulary
tree
wood
pencil

chair
paper towels
violin

This is a tree.

Wood comes from trees.

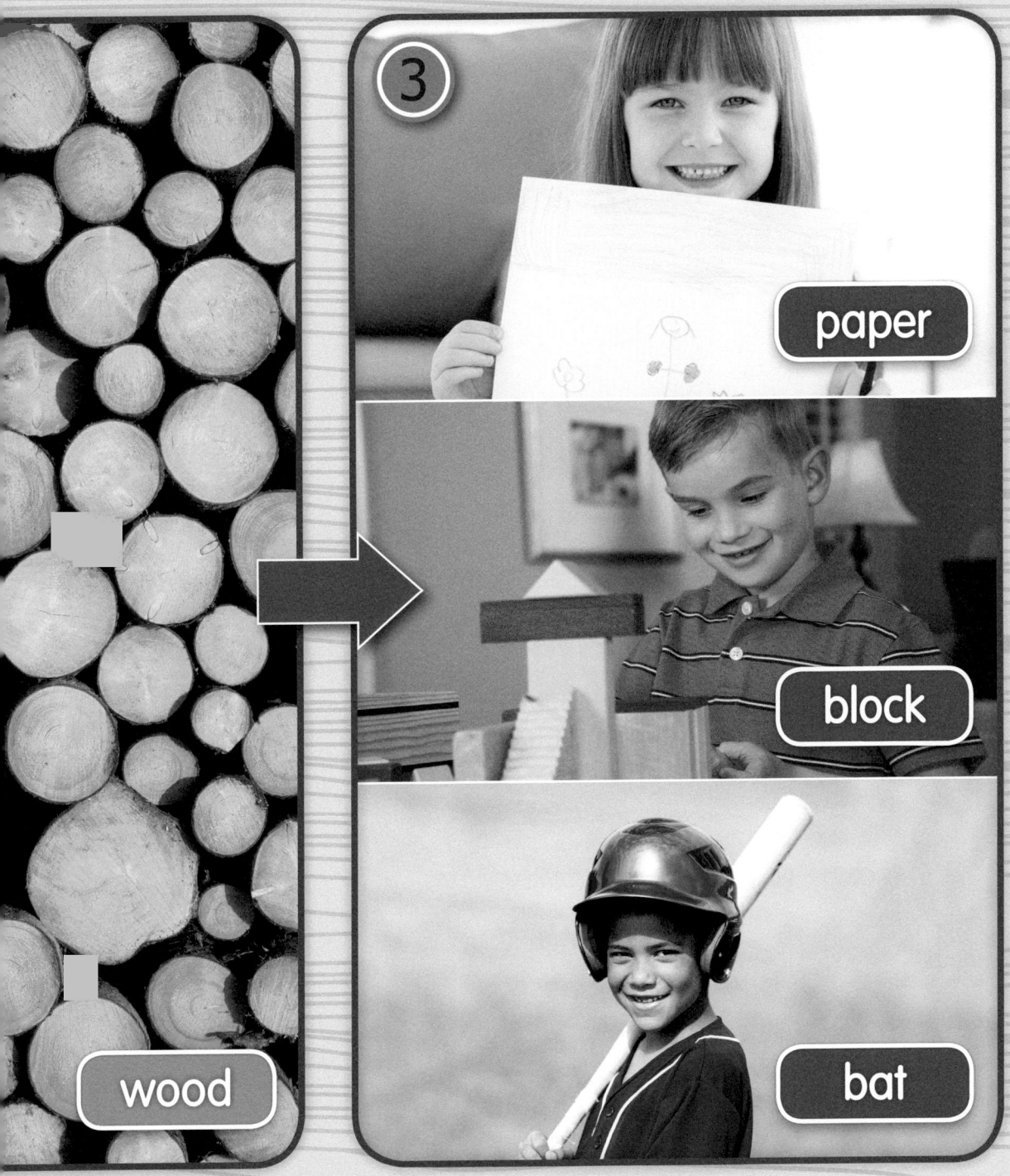

People use wood for many things.

A pencil is made of wood.
You write with a pencil.

A book is made from wood.
You read a book.

A chair is made of wood.
You sit on a chair.

Some houses are made of wood.
You live in a house.

Paper towels are made from wood. You clean with paper towels.

A violin is made of wood.
Can you play the violin?

Summary

These things are made of wood. What are they?

Song

Made of Wood

I live in a house that's made of wood,
Made of wood, made of wood.
I live in a house that's made of wood.
Wood comes from trees.

I read a book that's made from wood,
Made from wood, made from wood.
I read a book that's made from wood.
Wood comes from trees.

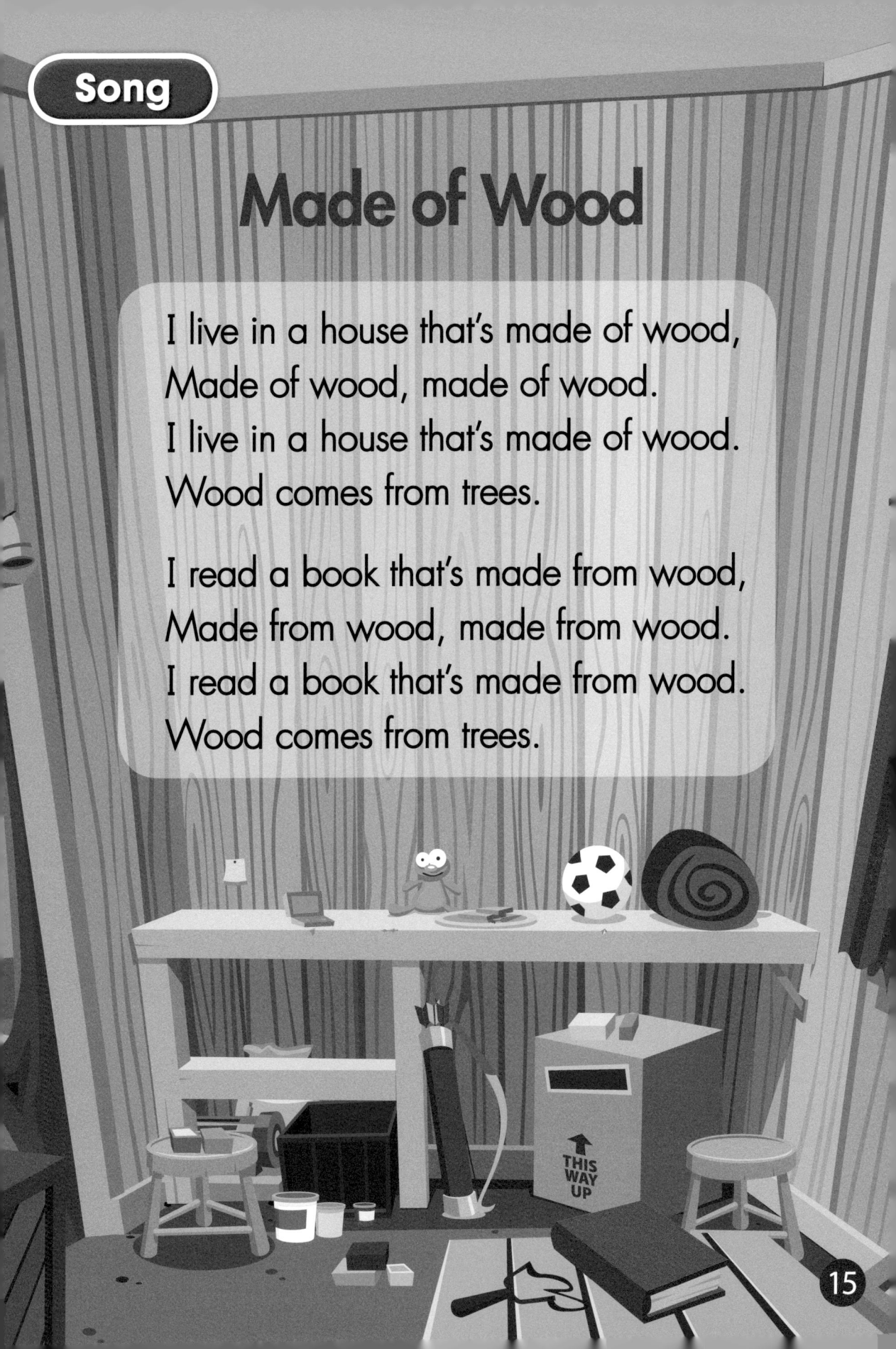

Index

bat, 7

block, 7

book, 9

chair, 10

house, 11

paper, 7

paper towels, 12

pencil, 8

tree, 6

violin, 13